D0914380

# The T♥ddler's handb☺☺k

### with over 100 Words
that every kid should know

BY DAYNA MARTIN

עִבְרִית / אַנְגְלִית

engage books
VANCOUVER

www.engagebooks.com

*Written & compiled by:* Dayna Martin
*Edited, designed & translated by:* A.R. Roumanis
*Proofread by:* Niv Hirsch ניב הירש
Judith Kimchi-Woods and Andrew Hickerson
*Photos supplied by:* Shutterstock
*Photo on page 47 by:* Faye Cornish

THIRD EDITION / THIRD PRINTING

LIBRARY AND ARCHIVES CANADA CATALOGUING IN PUBLICATION

Martin, Dayna, 1983–, author
   The toddler's handbook : numbers, colors, shapes, sizes, ABC animals,
opposites, and sounds, with over 100 words that every kid should know /
written by Dayna Martin ; edited by A.R. Roumanis.

Issued in print and electronic formats.
Text in English and Hebrew.
ISBN 978-1-77226-478-4 (bound). –
ISBN 978-1-77226-479-1 (paperback). –
ISBN 978-1-77226-480-7 (pdf). –
ISBN 978-1-77226-481-4 (epub). –
ISBN 978-1-77226-482-1 (kindle)

1. Hebrew language – Vocabulary – Juvenile literature.
2. Vocabulary – Juvenile literature.
3. Word recognition – Juvenile literature.
I. Martin, Dayna, 1983– . Toddler's handbook.
II. Martin, Dayna, 1983– . Toddler's handbook. Hebrew.
III. Title.

PJ4756.M37 2017          J492.4'81          C2017-905777-4          C2017-905778-2

**2**

אָלֶף בֵּית
Alef–Beyt
**ABCs** 4

מִסְפָּרִים
Misparim
**Numbers** 11

צְבָעִים
Tzvaim
**Colors** 14

נִיגוּדִים
Nigudim
**Opposites** 16

צוּרוֹת
Tzurot
**Shapes** 22

קוֹלוֹת
Kolot
**Sounds** 24

פְּעוּלוֹת
Peulot
**Actions** 28

רְגָשׁוֹת
Regashot
**Emotions** 30

סְפּוֹרְט
Sport
**Sports** 32

מְנוֹעִים
Meno'im
**Engines** 34

גְּדָלִים
G'dalim
**Sizes** 36

גּוּף
Guf
**Body** 38

כְּלֵי שׁוּלְחָן
Kley shulkhan
**Tableware** 40

בְּגָדִים
B'gadim
**Clothes** 42

זְמַן אַמְבַּטְיָה
Zman ambatyah
**Bath Time** 44

שְׁעַת הַשֵּׁנָה
She'at hashenah
**Bed Time** 45

3

# Aa

תַּנִין

Tanin

## Alligator

# Bb

דּוֹב

Dov

## Bear

# Cc

חָתוּל

Khatul

## Cat

כֶּלֶב
Kelev

Dd

# Dog

פִּיל
Pil

Ee

# Elephant

שׁוּעָל
Shu'al

# Fox

עֵז
Ez

Gg

# Goat 5

## Hh

סוּס

Sus

**Horse**

## Ii

אִיגוּאָנָה

Iguana

**Iguana**

יָגוּאָר

Yaguar

## Jj

**Jaguar**

6

## קוֹאָלָה
Ko'ala

# Kk

# Koala

## אַרְיֵה
Arye

# Ll

# Lion

## עַכְבָּר
Akhbar

# Mm

# Mouse

## נְיוּט
N'yut

# Nn

# Newt ל

## לוּטְרָה
### Lut'rah

# O o

## Otter

## חֲזִיר
### Kha'zir

# P p

## Pig

## שְׂלָיו
### Selav

# Q q

## 8  Quail

## אַרְנֶבֶת
### Arnevet

# R r

## Rabbit

כֶּלֶב יָם
Kelev Yam

# Ss

# Seal

נָמֵר
Na'mer

# Tt

# Tiger

אוּאַקְרִי
U'akari

# Uu

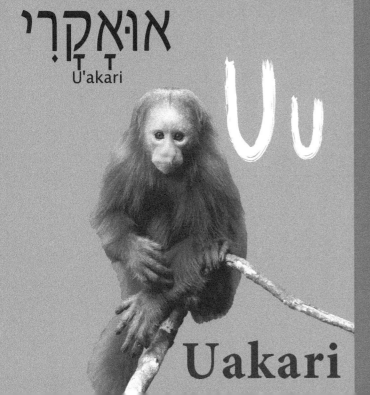

# Uakari

עַיִט
Ayit

# Vv

# Vulture 9

# Ww

סַמוּר

Samur

# Weasel

# Xx

דָג רֶנְטְגֶן

Dag rent'gn

# X-ray fish

# Yy

יָאק

Yak

10 **Yak**

# Zz

זֶבְּרָה

Zeb'rah

# Zebra

תַּפּוּחַ

Tapu'akh

אַחַת

Akhat

**1**

One

## Apple

קְרָקְרִים

Krekrerim

שְׁתַּיִם

Shtayim

**2**

Two

## Crackers

פְּרוּסוֹת אֲבַטִּיחַ

Prusot avatiyakh

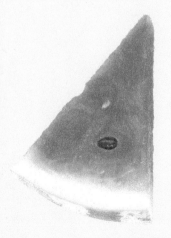

## Watermelon slices

11

תּוּתִים

Tutim

אַרְבַּע

Arba

4

Four

# Strawberries

גְּזָרִים

G'zarim

חָמֵשׁ

Khamesh

5

Five

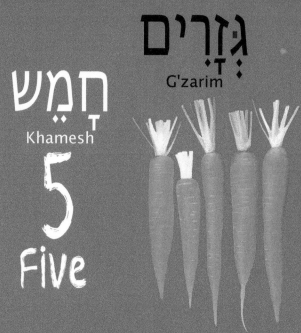

# Carrots

עַגְבָנִיּוֹת

Agvaniyot

שֵׁשׁ

Shesh

6

Six

# Tomatoes

# דְלַעוֹת
## D'la'ot

שֶׁבַע
Sheva

7

Seven

# Pumpkins

# פְּרוּסוֹת פְּרִי
## Prusot pri

שְׁמוֹנֶה
Shmoney

8

Eight

# Fruit slices

# תַּפּוּחֵי אֲדָמָה
## Tapukhey adamah

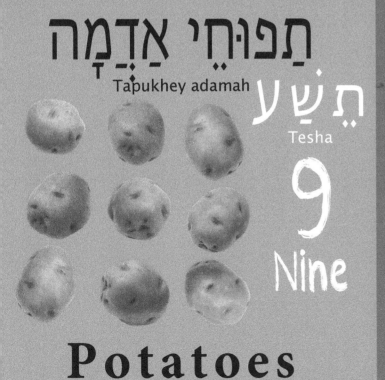

תֵּשַׁע
Tesha

9

Nine

# Potatoes

# עוּגִיּוֹת
## Ugiot

עֶשֶׂר
Eser

10

Ten

# Cookies   13

קֶשֶׁת בְּעָנָן
Keshet be'anan

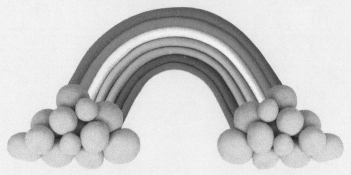

# Rainbow

אָדוֹם
Adom

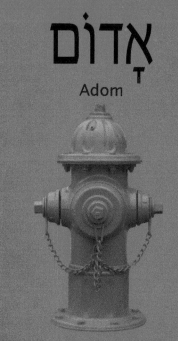

# Red

כָּתוֹם
Katom

14 **Orange**

צָהוֹב
Tzahov

# Yellow

יָרוֹק
Yarok

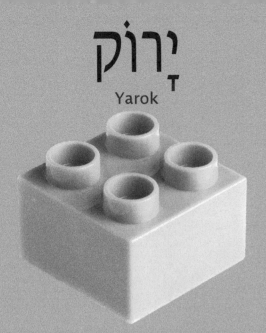

**Green**

כָּחֹל
Ka'khol

**Blue**

אִינְדִיגוֹ
Indigo

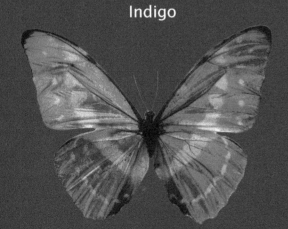

**Indigo**

סָגוֹל
Sagol

**Violet** 15

לְמַעְלָה
Le'malah

## Up

לְמַטָה
Le'matah

## Down

בְּ
Be

16 **In**

הַחוּצָה
Hakhutzah

**Out**

חַם

Ham

# Hot

קַר

Kar

# Cold

רָטוֹב

Ratov

# Wet

יָבֵשׁ

Yavesh

# Dry

17

מִלְפָנִים

Mil'fanim

**Front**

מֵאָחוֹר

Me'ahkhor

**Back**

דָלוּק

Daluk

18 **On**

כָּבוּי

Kabui

**Off**

פָּתוּחַ

Patu'akh

Open

סָגוּר

Sagur

Closed

רֵיק

Reyk

Empty

מָלֵא

Maleh

Full

19

בָּטוּחַ

Batu'akh

**Safe**

מְסוּכָּן

Mesukan

**Dangerous**

גָדוֹל

Gadol

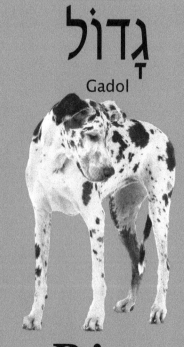

20 **Big**

קָטָן

Katan

**Small**

יָשֵׁן
Yashen

**Asleep**

עֵר
Ehr

**Awake**

אָרוֹךְ
Arokh

**Long**

קָצָר
Katzar

**Short**     21

מַעְגָּל

Ma'agal

# Circle

רִיבּוּעַ

Ribuah

# Square

מְשׁוּלָשׁ

Meshulash

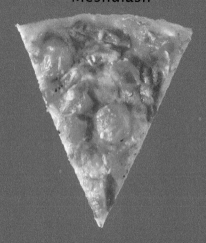

# 22 Triangle

מַלְבֵּן

Malben

# Rectangle

יָהֲלוֹם

Yahalom

# Diamond

כּוֹכָב

Kokhav

# Star

סְגַלְגַל

S'galgal

# Oval

לֵב

Lev

# Heart    23

## לְהִתְעַטֵּשׁ
Le'hit'a'tesh

אַפְּצִ'י!
Apchi!

*Ah-choo*

# Sneeze

## בַּרְוָז
Barvaz

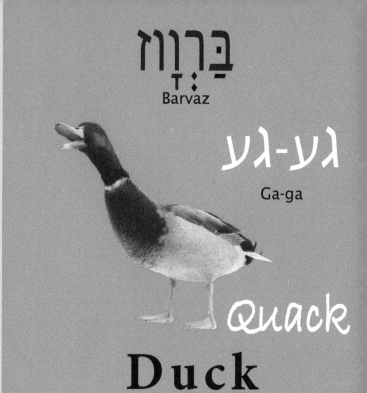

גַע-גַע
Ga-ga

*Quack*

# Duck

## פָּרָה
Para

מוווּ
Muuu

*Moo*

24 # Cow

## טֶלֶפוֹן
Tele'fon

צִלְצוּל
Tzil'zul

*Ring*

# Phone

קוֹף

Kof

אוּאוּ

Ooo-ooo

אַאַה

Ah-ah

Ooh-
ooh-
ahh-
ahh

# Monkey

צְפַרְדֵּעַ

Tzfarde'a

קווה קווה

Kwa kwa

*Ribbit*

# Frog

לְהַשְׁתִּיק

Le'hashtik

שְׁשְׁשׁ

Shhhh

*Shh*

# Hush

25

תַּרְנְגוֹל
Tarnegol

קוּקוּרִיקוּ
Kukuriku

Cock-a-
doodle-doo

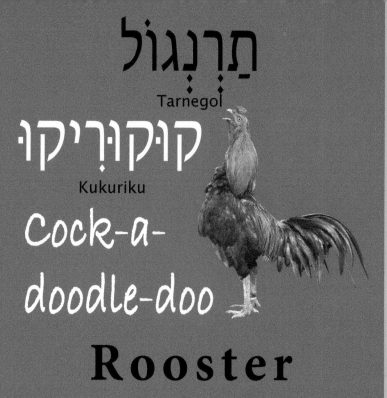

**Rooster**

תֻּפִּים
Tupim

בּוּם
Boum

Boom

**Drums**

נָחָשׁ
Nahash

סְסְס
Sss

Hiss

**Snake**

יַנְשׁוּף

Yanshuf

הוּ-הוּוּ

Hu-huuu

Hoot

## Owl

דְּבוֹרָה

D'vora

בְּזזז

Bzzz

Buzz

## Bumblebee

יָדַיִם

Yadayim

לִמְחוֹא

Limkho

Clap

## Hands

כֶּבֶשׂ

Keves

מֶה

Meh

Baa

## Sheep 27

לִזְחוֹל

Lizkhol

# Crawl

לְהִתְגַּלְגֵּל

Le'hitgalgel

# Roll

לָלֶכֶת

La'lekhet

28 **Walk**

לָרוּץ

La'roots

# Run

לִקְפּוֹץ
Likpotz

# Hop

לִרְכּוֹב
Lirkov

# Ride

לְנַשֵׁק
Le'nashek
# Kiss

לִקְפּוֹץ
Likpotz
# Jump    29

## שָׂמֵחַ
Same'akh

# Happy

## עָצוּב
Atzuv

# Sad

## כּוֹעֵס
Ko'es

30 # Angry

## פּוֹחֵד
Pokhed

# Scared

מְתֻסְכָּל

Metuskal

# Frustrated

מוּפְתָּע

Mufta

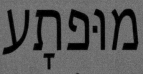

# Surprised

בֶּהֱלֶם

B'helem

# Shocked

אַמִּיץ

Amitz

# Brave 31

בֵּיסְבּוֹל

Beysbol

# Baseball

כַּדוּרְסַל

Kadur'sal

# Basketball

טֶנִיס

Tenis

32 Tennis

כַּדוּרֶגֶל

Kaduregel

# Soccer

נוֹצִית

Notzit

# Badminton

פּוּטְבּוֹל

Futbol

# Football

כַּדּוּר עָף

Kadur af

# Volleyball

גּוֹלְף

Golf

# Golf   33

כַּבָּאִית

Kaba'it

# Fire truck

אוֹטוֹ

Oto

מַשָּׂאִית

Masa'it

34 **Car**

**Truck**

מָסוֹק

Masok

# Helicopter

מָטוֹס

Matos

# Airplane

רַכֶּבֶת

Rakevet

# Train

סִירָה

Siira

# Boat 35

קָטָן
Katan

בֵּינוֹנִי
Beynoni

גָּדוֹל
Gadol

# Small    Medium    Large

קָטָן
Katan

בֵּינוֹנִי
Beynoni

גָּדוֹל
Gadol

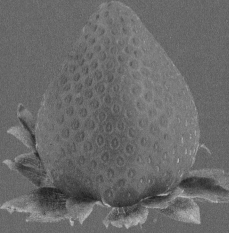

# 36 Small Medium    Large

גָּדוֹל
Gadol

בֵּינוֹנִי
Beynoni

קָטָן
Katan

**Large** **Medium** **Small**

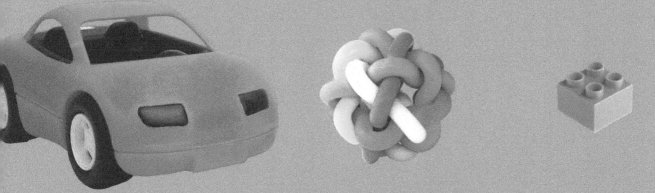

גָּדוֹל
Gadol

בֵּינוֹנִי
Beynoni

קָטָן
Katan

**Large** **Medium** **Small** 37

רֹאשׁ

Rosh

# Head

כְּתֵפַיִם

Ktefayim

# Shoulders

בִּרְכַּיִם

Birkayim

# Knees

אֶצְבָּעוֹת רַגְלַיִם

Etzba'ot raglayim

# Toes

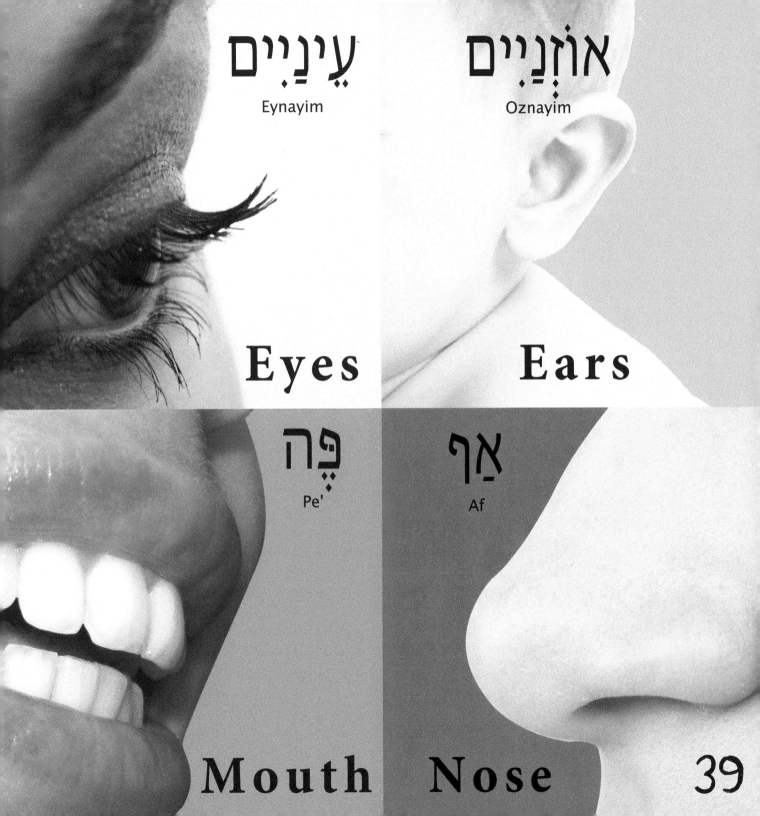

עֵינַיִים
Eynayim

Eyes

אוֹזְנַיִים
Oznayim

Ears

פֶּה
Pe'

Mouth

אַף
Af

Nose

39

כּוֹס סְפִּי

Kos sipi

# Sippy cup

קְעָרָה

Ke'ara

# Bowl

סִיר

Seyr

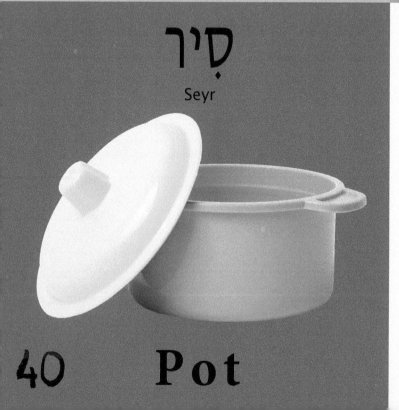

40 **Pot**

כּוֹס

Kos

# Cup

## צֶלַחַת
Tzalakhat

Plate

## מַזְלֵג
Mazleg

Fork

## סַכִּין
Sakin

Knife

## כַּף
Kaf

Spoon 41

כּוֹבַע

Kova

**Hat**

חוּלְצָה

Khultza

**Shirt**

מִכְנָסַיִים

Mikhnasayim

42 **Pants**

מִכְנָסַיִים קְצָרִים

Mikhnasayim ktzarim

**Shorts**

## כְּפָפוֹת
Kfafot

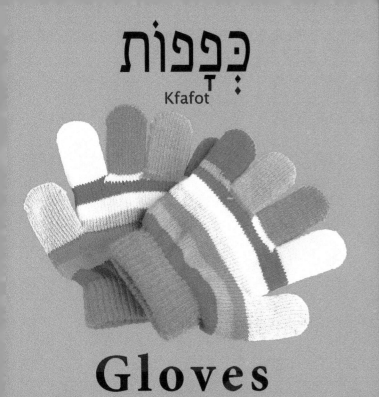

# Gloves

## מִשְׁקְפֵי שֶׁמֶשׁ
Mishk'fey shemesh

# Sunglasses

## גַּרְבַּיִם
Garbayim

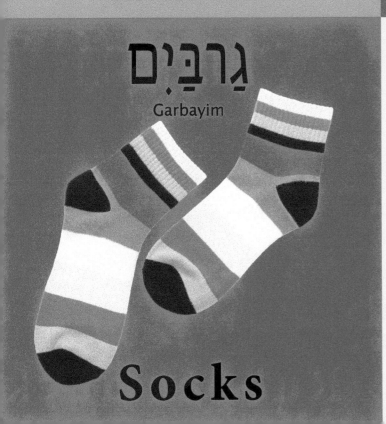

# Socks

## נַעֲלַיִם
Na'alayim

# Shoes    43

זְמָן אַמְבַּטְיָה
Zman ambatya

Bath time

אַמְבַּטְיָה
Ambatya

**Bath**

סַבּוֹן
Sabon

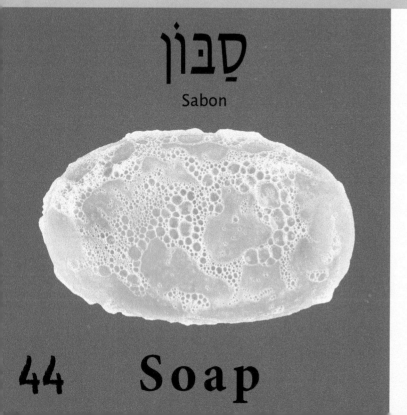

44 **Soap**

בַּרְוָז גּוּמִי
Barvaz gumi

**Rubber duck**

## לְצַחְצֵחַ שִׁנַיִם
Le'tzakh'tze'akh Shinayim

# Brush teeth

## שְׁעַת הַשֵּׁנָה
She'at hashenah

## סֵפֶר
Sefer

*Bed time*

# Book

## סִיר לַיְלָה
Seer layla

# Potty

## מִיטָה
Mita

# Bed 45

# THE Toddler's handbook

## activity / פְּעִילוּת
Pe'ilut

Match the following to the pictures below.
Can you find **7 pumpkins**, a hooting owl,
a rainbow, a baseball, a lion, square blocks,
a sad boy, a helicopter, and shoes?

הַתְאִימוּ אֶת הַמִּילִים הַבָּאוֹת לַתְּמוּנוֹת שֶׁמִּתַּחַת.

הַאִם תּוּכְלוּ לִמְצוֹא: דְּלַעַת, יַנְשׁוּף, קֶשֶׁת בֶּעָנָן,

בֵּיסְבּוֹל, אַרְיֵה, קוּבִּיּוֹת, יֶלֶד עָצוּב, מַסוֹק וְנַעֲלַיִם?

מַסוֹק
Masok

helicopter

נַעֲלַיִם
Na'alayim

shoes

יַנְשׁוּף
Yanshuf

hooting owl

בֵּיסְבּוֹל
beysbol

baseball

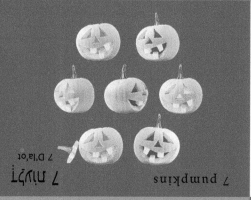

7 דְּלָעוֹת
7 D'la'ot

7 pumpkins

יֶלֶד עָצוּב
Yeled atzuv

sad boy

46

אַרְיֵה
Aryeh

lion

קוּבִּיּוֹת
Kubeyot

square blocks

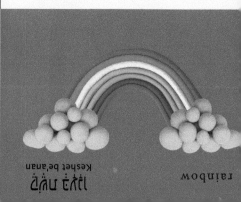

קֶשֶׁת בֶּעָנָן
keshet be'anan

rainbow

# Find more early concept books at www.engagebooks.com

## About the Author

Dayna Martin is the mother of three young boys. When she finished writing *The Toddler's Handbook* her oldest son was 18 months old, and she had newborn twins. Following the successful launch of her first book, Dayna began work on *The Baby's Handbook, The Preschooler's Handbook,* and *The Kindergartener's Handbook.* The ideas in her books were inspired by her search to find better ways to teach her children. The concepts were vetted by numerous educators in different grade levels. Dayna is a stay-at-home mom, and is passionate about teaching her children in innovative ways. Her experiences have inspired her to create resources to help other families. With thousands of copies sold, and translations in more than twenty five different languages, her books have already become a staple learning source for many children around the world.

## Translations

| | |
|---|---|
| ARMENIAN | ITALIAN |
| ASL (SIGN) | JAPANESE |
| ARABIC | KOREAN |
| CANTONESE | MANDARIN |
| DUTCH | PERSIAN |
| ENGLISH | POLISH |
| FILIPINO | PORTUGUESE |
| FRENCH | PUNJABI |
| GERMAN | RUSSIAN |
| GREEK | SPANISH |
| HEBREW | TELUGU |
| HINDI | VIETNAMESE |

*Have comments or suggestions?*
*Contact us at: alexis@engagebooks.ca*

Show us how you enjoy your **#handbook**. Tweet a picture to **@engagebooks** for a chance to win free prizes.

47

CPSIA information can be obtained
at www.ICGtesting.com
Printed in the USA
BVHW021938250421
605737BV00030B/329